What Do You Think of You?

and other thoughts on self-esteem

Scott Sheperd, Ph.D.

CompCare® Publishers

Minneapolis, Minnesota

Library of Congress Cataloging-in-Publication Data

Sheperd, Scott, 1945-
    What do you think of you? / by Scott Sheperd
        p. cm.
    Summary: Discusses the importance of self-esteem, particularly
during the teenage years, how it can be developed, and options for
dealing with fears and problems in adolescence.
    ISBN 0-89638-220-6
    1. Self–respect in adolescence—Juvenile literature.
2. Teenagers—Conduct of life. [1. Self-respect. 2. Adolescence.]
I. Title
BF724.3.S36S43 1990   90-38201
158'.1'0835—dc20   CIP
                               AC

Illustrations by Harry Pulver, Jr.
Cover and interior design by MacLean & Tuminelly

Inquiries, orders, and catalog requests should be addressed to
CompCare Publishers
2415 Annapolis Lane
Minneapolis, Minnesota 55441
Call toll free 800/328-3330
(Minnesota residents 612/559-4800)

5	4	3	2	1
94	93	92	91	90

Contents

Introduction

You're in Charge Here!

You're in Charge Here!

Although I often talk with junior and senior high school students about self-esteem, it's a problem that affects people of all ages. Adults shake their heads sadly about the low self-esteem of today's young people, but the truth is, a great many of them don't have healthy self-esteem either.

When people don't feel good about themselves, their general attitude is negative. They see everything in life through dark glasses, colored somewhere between grey and black.

People with a negative attitude pass it on to others....Older teen-agers give it to younger ones....Parents pass it on to their children....Teachers hand it out to their students....Bosses dish it out to employees....Employees take it home and share it with their families.

All this happens when people have low self-esteem.

Contrary to what many advertisers want us to believe, self-esteem has nothing to do with designer clothes, expensive cars, or good looks. Having healthy self-esteem means that, on a very deep level, you believe you're basically a good person (but not perfect!) and that you have value as a human being.

How can you find self-esteem if you don't have it? How can you raise your self-image if it's unhappily low? That's what this little book is about.

However, one of the most important things you can learn is—who's in charge of how you feel about yourself? The answer is YOU ARE! Think about it for a minute — can anyone else possibly make you feel a certain way if you don't want to?

Other people may have a profoundly important effect on your mood or attitude and some of you are up against over-whelming odds in situations so tough the rest of us can barely comprehend. Never-theless, it's still true: no one can force you to feel anything—good or bad! So, if somebody says, "Hey, you're a real loser!" you may or may not get angry, but you won't feel like a loser unless you already agree! Eleanor Roosevelt once said, "No one can make you feel inferior without your permission."

On the other hand, if someone takes you by the shoulders and says, "Hey, kid, you better get some self-esteem or you'll miss out on all the good stuff!" that won't help either. You can't feel good unless you want to.

You alone are responsible for your feelings. YOU'RE IN CHARGE HERE!

Everyone has down times. Every teen-ager and pre-teen, every adult —EVERYONE— struggles with insecurities, fear of disapproval, doubts about his or her physical appearance, etc. This is a natural part of being a thinking, caring, feeling human being. The struggle to resolve these fears and self-doubts actually helps you build up emotional coping "muscles" and also strong self-esteem.

Once in awhile people get so stuck feeling down that they run out of hope. They can't see anything good about themselves or their lives and can't find any reason to look forward to tomorrow. All they can see is another day of pain.

If you're that person, or if you know some-one who is, you need to get special advice from a professional helper right away. Your pain is very real, but it will not last forever. There's a phone number at the back of this book you can call night or day and talk to other teen-agers or adults who understand what you're going through.

They can help you get unstuck. Also, be sure to read the chapter here called, "Wait Till You Can See Tomorrow."

There's one question that may have occurred to you by now: If everyone has problems with self-esteem, why write a book just for teens? Well, as one psychologist said, "Adolescence is the equivalent of normal, temporary insanity." In other words, it's tough, real tough. In fact, even though most parents don't want to admit it, it's tougher now than it's ever been.

The pressures over drugs, alcohol, and sex are greater than ever. Our society, in general, is much more permissive than it's ever been, and that permissiveness is especially dangerous for young people.

It's also confusing, as a teen-ager, to be encouraged to grow up instantly, but at the same time, "just say no" to something like drinking that you see glamorized as an adult thing to do.

Obviously, the teen years are challenging times. But, along with the challenge comes freedom. Your attitudes and feelings are entirely up to you, and you are free to become the kind of person you want to be.

Now is your time.

This is your Self.

You're in charge here!

-1-

What Do You Think of You?

Ideas for Building Self-esteem

"*Where do I go to look up the meaning of my life?*"

— Anonymous

Talk show hosts say the best TV interviews come from kids under 10 and women over 70.

That's because these people will tell you the plain, unvarnished truth!

"Never be afraid to stand alone."

— Douglas Hesse, 8

You can see this in an elementary school classroom. Try asking some children, "What do you think of you?"

There'll be enthusiastic answers right away. "Wow, I'm a 9!" or "Not me. I'm a 10!"

■

"We live in a culture that tells us to expect happiness. If we aren't happy, then there must be something wrong with us! But this is not a realistic expectation. Real life is full of surprises. You will have good days and bad days. You will be happy sometimes and unhappy sometimes."

—Gershen Kaufman, Ph.D., Lev Raphael, Ph.D.
*Stick Up for Yourself: Every Kid's Guide to
Personal Power and Positive Self-Esteem*

■

When kids get older, they aren't as sure of themselves anymore.

What about you, for instance? On the scale of 1 to 10, how would you rate yourself right now? Would you choose a safe, middle-of-the-road number like 5?

Or maybe you really feel like a 3 or a 2 — or worse.

"Ninety percent of the way you feel is determined by how you want to feel and how you expect to feel."

—John Kozak

What happened to the self-esteem you once had?

For one thing, you became conscious of yourself in ways you never noticed before. Then you began looking around at other people and comparing yourself to them.

That's when you started to worry about your "rating."

*"The deepest principle in human nature is
the craving to be appreciated."*

— William James

Do you measure up to the others?

Maybe you do, maybe you don't — and if you don't, what then?

Does that mean no one will like you? Will you have to go through the rest of your life with no friends?

Some people are so uncomfortable with this uncertainty they'll do just about anything to make sure they fit in.

"*It is not because things are difficult that we do not dare; it is because we do not dare that they are difficult.*"

— Seneca

Once you've realized you could be a "social failure," you begin to experience a very powerful emotion.

FEAR

Fear grows directly out of these new doubts about yourself — and then turns back on you to add to the pain.

"It's not hard to find the truth. What is hard is not to run away from it once you have found it."

— Etienne Gilson

Fear is a killer!

Fear kills love... humor... enthusiasm...
warmth... growth... curiosity... adventure...
creativity... sensitivity... understanding...
compassion.

"Never turn your back on a threatened danger and try to run away from it. If you do that, you will double the danger. But if you meet it promptly and without flinching, you will reduce the danger by half."

— Winston Churchill

Fear kills the spirit!

It can kill your spirit, too.

And fear is everywhere — high school,
junior high, the business world —
everywhere.

*"Fear has a thousand voices,
A thousand reasons why,
A thousand ways to bind us,
But fear always lies."*

— Robbie Gass

There are all kinds of fear.

Fear of being laughed at
Fear of being different
Fear of being left out
Fear of appearing too smart
Fear of being stupid
Fear of being rejected
Fear of success
Fear of failure
Fear of being weak
Fear of being alone

"Worry is a thin stream of fear trickling through the mind. If encouraged, it cuts a channel into which all other thoughts are drained."

— Arthur Somers Roche

With all these worries, you might feel like
you're swimming in fear!

(Maybe drowning.)

■

*"If we choose to run scared,
our capacity for love is limited."*

— Sheldon Kopp

■

Constantly being stressed by fear is truly exhausting.

Soon you're so emotionally worn down that nothing in life looks very good anymore.

"*Positive anything is better than negative nothing.*"

— Elbert Hubbard

The true, light-hearted sense of fun is gone.

In its place, there's forced laughter and making fun of others.

There's also the artificial "fun" of partying with mood-altering drugs and alcohol, followed by a high price to pay.

■

"To the extent you hide your feelings, you are alienated from yourself and others. And your loneliness is proportional."

— Dorothy Briggs

■

Enthusiasm disappears — or at least it gets controlled.

You can only be enthusiastic at designated times, so there's no risk of looking different or weird.

*"There's so much good in the worst of us
and so much bad in the best of us
that it's hard to tell which of us
ought to reform the rest of us."*

— Ogden Nash

With all the complicated, new stresses
in your life, it's easy to lose your self-
confidence.

If it's any comfort, you're certainly not
alone. Everyone goes through these self-
doubts. It's a miserable time.

■

"But, if I tell you who I am, you may not like who I am, and it is all I have."

— John Powell, S.R.

■

These doubts can cause pretty serious confusion, and there doesn't seem to be any easy answer — just more questions.

The big question is, how could others possibly like you if they knew all about you — your weaknesses, imperfections, warts and all?

If people knew *everything*, they'd reject you — wouldn't they?

That's the Ultimate Fear.

"The battle to keep up appearances unnecessarily, the mask — whatever name you give creeping perfectionism — robs us of our energies."

— Robin Worthington

It's so scary to expose your real self and risk rejection that very few people will take that chance.

If you're like most of us, you hide your real feelings to protect yourself. Then you put up a fake front and do a lot of pretending.

This also gets very tiring, but what other choice do you have?

*"We spend so much time disguising our-
selves from everybody that we end up
disguising ourselves from ourselves."*

— François de Rochefocauld

So, you keep up appearances and try to win approval from your friends. You're careful not to make any stupid mistakes and you laugh at things you don't think are funny. You're doing everything you think you should, but something isn't working.

You were trying to feel better about yourself, but now you're feeling worse.

You were hoping to regain your confidence. Now you're even less sure of yourself.

*"We know what happens to people
who stay in the middle of the road;
they get run over."*

— Aneurin Bevan

It seems like the harder you've tried to please everybody, the less you're pleased with yourself.

It's a vicious cycle.

"Never...deny your own experience or conviction."

— Dag Hammarskjöld

People who feel trapped in this vicious cycle also feel

desperate,
hopeless,
a desire to escape.

They're like an accident waiting to happen.

The odds are pretty great that you know someone like this.

"*When someone demands blind obedience, you'd be a fool not to peek.*"

— Jim Feibig

People who feel trapped will try anything to escape.

They'll try life-and-death things like

    substance abuse,
    high-risk sexual activity,
    drinking and driving,
    suicide.

"Still around the corner there may wait a new road or a secret gate."

— J.R.R. Tolkien

Do you feel trapped?

"If you get some hard bumps, it at least shows you are out of the rut."

— Anonymous

You don't have to be.

You don't have to stay stuck.

There is a way out.

"*Some doors once opened, can never be fully closed again. Take care to only open doors you are willing to pass through.*"

— Norm Howe

In a story called, "The Lady and the Tiger," a man was forced to choose between two doors to gain his freedom. Behind one door was a tiger and certain death. Behind the other was a lady and the path to freedom.

This poor man's predicament was that he had no idea which door was which, so how would he decide the right one to choose?

*"Everybody, sooner or later, sits down to
a banquet of consequences."*

— Robert Louis Stevenson

In real life, we all face choices like the one in the story. But, most of the doors we face with "tigers" behind them have big danger signs attached: "Don't open me!"

"Don't drink and drive!"

"Don't do drugs!"

In spite of the warnings, people (young and old) still go ahead and open the dangerous doors. Do you ever wonder why?

*"Those who look for reasons to hate
miss opportunities to love."*

— Carmen Sylva

Many adults blame teen-agers' choices on peer pressure. The way they talk about it, you'd think that Peers are little people from outer space, who land for a while, talk kids into opening the wrong doors, then get back in their spaceship and take off for Planet Peer.

"I have never met a man who has given me as much trouble as I have given myself."

— Dwight L. Moody

That isn't how peer pressure works.
The real pressure doesn't come from your
friends, egging you on.

The most powerful force comes from
inside you, because more than anything,
you want to be approved of and loved.

"It is vain to hope to please all alike. Let a man stand with his face in what direction he will, he must necessarily turn his back on one-half of the world."

— Anonymous

For those of you who feel trapped or stuck with low self-esteem, there is a way to get free.

You wanted to feel good about yourself, so you tried to win approval from your friends, right?

What went wrong?

"There's nothing wrong with needing and wanting someone to like us....We get in trouble only when we do not like ourselves and as a result make mistakes trying to force others to like us."

— Eugene Kennedy

Maybe your mistake was changing yourself to please these other people. Maybe when you were trying to meet their expectations, you had to give up your own.

If that's what happened, it was like opening a door to danger, only instead of facing a tiger, there was quicksand.

"*A man who trims himself to suit every-body will soon whittle himself away.*"

— Charles M. Schwab

Slowly but surely, you found yourself sinking.

Everytime you changed or compromised or gave yourself up, your self-esteem got lower and lower.

■

*"The doors we open and close each day
decide the lives we live."*

— Flora Whittemore

■

Luckily, it's not too late for a second chance!

You can choose another door.

Which one will it be?

■

*"The world is all gates, all opportunities,
strings of tension waiting to be strung."*

— Ralph Waldo Emerson

■

There are many doors to choose from, and some will lead to attractive things, such as money, success, and fame.

These may be nice to have, but they don't guarantee good feelings.

■

*"Two roads diverged in the woods
and I —
I took the one less traveled by,
And that has made all the difference."*

— Robert Frost

■

There's only one way to find real
self-esteem and that's on the path you
follow when you're true to yourself.

*"A respect for our own existence despite
our defects...is one of the most liberating
experiences life can offer."*

— Eugene Kennedy

That's also the only way to find
personal freedom.

■

*"The self of experience is reliable even
though it is imperfect or unfinished. We
can trust it and find our way into love
and friendship through it. Listening to
our true self is a way of really loving
ourselves. And it makes it possible for
others to love us as well."*

— Eugene Kennedy

■

And self-esteem happens to be the first step to finding the love you're looking for.

■

"Integrity simply means a willingness not to violate one's identity."

— Erich Fromm

■

If you're true to yourself, you'll feel good about yourself.

You'll feel good about yourself if you're true to yourself.

It works both ways.

"Serenity is a gift from you to you."

— Dorothy Briggs

All along, you've held the key.

No other person's approval will ever feel good enough — unless you approve of yourself first.

■

"When you play your own game, people you like will join your team."

— Susu Levy

■

If every single one of your friends swears that you're a total "10"... if you earn straight A's every semester... even if you drive a red Porsche to school, you won't feel that solid, center core of self-esteem unless...

... you give yourself permission to be your real self;

... you get comfortable with your self, including all your personal strengths and weaknesses.

"True goodness springs from a man's own heart. All men are born good."

— Confucius

In his book, *If You Really Knew Me,
Would You Still Like Me?* Dr. Eugene
Kennedy says that our difficulties don't
lie in the untrusting world around us, but
in our own failure to trust in the goodness
and value of what is within us.

■

"Do not let what you cannot do interfere with what you can."

— John Wooden

■

Self-esteem doesn't mean that

> you're a "10" in looks
> or physical dimensions;

> you've got it all together
> all the time;

> you've accomplished wonders.

In the whole world there are probably
only 2 or 3 people with all this — if that
many.

"Nobody's life is smooth and easy. Everybody has ups and downs. We've got to expect that. Indeed, we may even be eager to try ourselves out, to discover how capable we really are."

— Louis Bisch

Self-esteem does mean that

  you believe in your worth and value
  as a human being;

  you accept your limitations and
  acknowledge your good qualities, too.

"To learn, you must want to be taught."

— Proverbs 12:1

If you are going to discover your own true richness and avoid following the unproductive paths taken by many young people, you'll need some special things.

■

"Everyone has talent. What is rare is the courage to follow the talent to the places where it leads."

— Erica Jong

■

You'll need

> courage,
> openness,
> curiosity,
> silence.

"To be nobody but yourself, in a world which is doing its best to make you everybody else, means to fight the hardest battle which any human being can fight, and never stop fighting."

— e.e. cummings

Courage is needed to be honest with yourself, to understand yourself, and to become aware of your relationship to the rest of the world.

It takes courage to stand apart.

It takes courage to be yourself.

It takes courage to make your own choices.

"Receiving messages opens our minds, our hearts, and our futures."

— Joe Tanenbaum

Openness is critical, because a mind
that is closed will stay stuck with the old,
fearful ways.

Being open means you are willing to
consider new information and new ideas.
Like sun and water to a plant, openness
allows you to learn and grow.

■

"Throughout the centuries there were men who took first steps down new roads, armed with nothing but their own vision."

— Ayn Rand

■

Curiosity sounds like it's something just for children. Not true! Curiosity is a vital quality for people of all ages. Some of the most curious people become scientists and inventors.

You'll need curiosity to learn what your options are, to explore the exciting possibilities that exist.

Curiosity breeds adventure and discovery — not just of things, but of the magic of being alive.

■

"Stillness and tranquillity set things in order in the universe."

— Tao Te Ching

■

Silence, strange as it may seem, is an equally important addition to this list. Most of us are uncomfortable with silence. We prefer some kind of noise going on.

But we also need silence.

■

*"Silence is a true friend
who never betrays."*

— Confucius

■

In moments of silence, we can...

...clear our head and just be;

...learn how to listen peacefully;

..."nurture silence in a noisy heart" so we can listen to our own voice from within.

"Only when you drink from the river of silence shall you indeed sing."

— Kahlil Gibran

Silence is not just
the absence of noise.

It is one of the essential
nutrients of our lives.

"To wait for someone to do something for you contributes to the lessening of your own self-esteem."

— Dorothy Briggs

There are no ready-made road maps
through life that point out all the pitfalls,
potholes, and doors with danger behind
them.

You'll have to take the initiative and find
your own way.

When you need help, you'll have to ask
for it.

"There are really only two ways to approach life — as a victim or as a gallant fighter — and you must decide if you want to act or react. If you don't decide which way to play with life, it always plays with you."

— Merle Shain

You're in charge here.

You're in charge of your attitude
and feelings.

You have to risk facing your weaknesses
so you can celebrate your strengths.

You are responsible for your self-esteem.

■

"You have brains in your head.
You have feet in your shoes.
You can steer yourself
any direction you choose."

— Dr. Seuss,
Oh, The Places You'll Go!

■

No other person is responsible for your happiness. That job has been assigned to you.

You have to ask questions to identify your options.

You have to make your own choices and then take action.

"I have always been delighted at the prospect of a new day, a fresh try, one more start, with perhaps a bit of magic waiting somewhere behind the morning."

— J. B. Priestley

Today is a good time to make
a new beginning.

"Let love be your greatest aim."

— 1 Corinthians 14:1

Explore what love is.

Don't just accept what others tell you.

"The ones who get on in this world are the ones who get up and look for the circumstances they want, and if they can't find them, make them."

— George Bernard Shaw

Explore what success means.

Don't just listen to what the
TV commercials say.

"Life does not require us to make good; it asks only that we give our best at each new level of experience."

— Harold Ruopp

What does it mean to fail?

Are you a failure if you fail at something?

Question it. Think about it.

*"Kindness in words creates confidence.
Kindness in thinking creates
profoundness.
Kindness in feeling creates love."*

— Lao Tzu

Be part of building up, not tearing down.

Look around for ways you might be negative toward others. Is that what you want to be doing?

You can make a different choice if you want to.

*"Live your best, think your best,
and do your best today,
for today will soon be tomorrow
and tomorrow will soon be forever."*

— A. P. Gouthey

This is your time. This is your Now.

You're in charge of your Self.

What kind of person do you want to be?

What do you *want* to think of you?

-2-

Wait Till You Can See Tomorrow

Thoughts When Life Has Too Much Pain

"Our greatest glory is not in never falling, but in rising every time we fall."

— Confucius

Some young people are literally over-whelmed by intense emotional pain. Maybe you're one of them.

Maybe your life circumstances are more difficult than anyone knows — so threatening, frightening, or filled with shame that you can't talk about it with anyone.

Maybe your own self-esteem is rock-bottom low because you've made such a mess of things it would kill your parents to tell them.

Maybe you've started thinking about ending your own life instead.

"You have seen me tossing and turning through the night. You have collected my tears and preserved them in your bottle! The very day I call for help...this one thing I know: God is for me!"

— Psalm 56:8-9

Stop and listen!

■

*"Relieve the distress of my heart, free me
from my sufferings."*

— Psalm 25:17

■

Your pain is very real. It probably starts as soon as you wake up in the morning and won't go away till you can sleep again.

Emotional pain causes physical pain too. All the muscles in your body may feel like they're burning. You could feel dizzy or numb, like you can just barely move. You may be near tears many times during the day.

■

"No one ever fools you as constantly and as successfully as you fool yourself."

— Dr. Paul Parker

■

Your feelings are real and you have a right to feel them.

But your thinking is wrong. You've become confused because you're emotionally and physically exhausted.

Ending your life is not a rational act. There are other ways to end the pain.

Wait and see.

■

"Everyone takes the limits of his own field of vision for the limits of the world."

— Schopenhauer

■

Right now you're like a person driving a car while lost in thick fog.

Destroying the car because you can't see where to drive doesn't make sense.

There are other, rational answers.

■

"The darkest night since the beginning of time did not turn out all the stars."

— Anonymous

■

What you need to find is a ray of light, a small break of light to guide you through the fog.

The fog rolled in, and it's as thick and dark as night, but the sun didn't go away.

"Behind the night, somewhere afar, some white, tremendous daybreak!"

— Rupert Brooke

Even though the chilling cold of this dark, foggy night has temporarily confused you, deep in your heart you know some important truths.

The sun is still there, and it always will be.

The fog will eventually pass, too, because it always does.

■

*"Far away there in the sunshine are my
highest aspirations. I may not reach
them, but I can look up and see their
beauty, believe in them, and try
to follow where they lead."*

— Louisa May Alcott

■

Can you remember a time, maybe weeks or months or years ago, when you could see the sunshine?

Can you remember how you felt then?

Grab those remembered feelings right now and hold on to them as hard as you can.

"It is only with the heart that one can see rightly; what is essential is invisible to the eye."

— Antoine de Saint-Exupéry

Good feelings will come again.

But sometimes there are no fast answers.

"It is the first law of friendship that it be cultivated; the second law is to be indulgent when the first law has been neglected."

— Voltaire

You might reach out to a counselor
at school and find that you are not
understood.

You might reach out to friends and they
won't hear you.

*"Peace I leave with you; my peace
I give to you....Do not let your hearts be
troubled and do not be afraid."*

— John 14:27

If you believe in God, you might reach out in prayer and not sense an answer.

"The greatest problem of communication is the illusion that it has been accomplished."

— George Bernard Shaw

Part of the communication breakdown could be coming from you. Maybe you aren't able to see or hear the care that is coming to you.

Intense emotional pain actually affects all your senses. Food doesn't even taste good when you feel this way.

"Depression is the great deceiver."

— Arnold Beisser

Still, ending your life is not the answer.

■

"Life can hurt us, but it does not hurt nearly so much if we have learned to listen to ourselves and to recognize how fully and richly we are trying to tell ourselves the truth."

— Eugene Kennedy

■

Make believe, for just a moment, that you are someone else. Pretend that you are your very best friend. As this friend, you've been told all the scary or shameful secrets and you've tried as hard as you can to understand your friend's pain.

What would you tell your best friend to do?

Take that advice.

That's the voice of your real, inner self taking care of you.

"We are each of us angels with only one wing. And we can fly only by embracing each other."

— Luciano de Crescenzo

Allow yourself to be loved — by yourself, your loved ones, and your friends.

■

"Mistakes are a fact of life. It's the response to the error that counts."

— Nikki Giovanni

■

Forgive yourself for not being perfect.

Forgive yourself for feeling guilty, for being sad, for feeling pain.

■

*"Most problems precisely defined are
already partially solved."*

— Harry Lorayne

■

Ask for help!

Call for it!

Call a crisis hotline for young people.
A phone number is listed at the back of
this book.

"Purpose gives you energy."

— Anonymous

You must also take action.

Remember that you are responsible for yourself, so when you do take action, give yourself credit — even if it's just a very small step forward.

"If we do the duty next to us and then the duty next to that, light begins to break on life's ultimate issues."

— Dr. Robert W. Stockman

Keep busy, even with routine tasks, like cleaning your room, or making lists of things you will do when you feel better.

Write letters to yourself so you can look back on this time and remember the emotional survival skills you're learning.

Help someone else — a child or an elderly person.

■

*"Normal day, let me be aware of the
treasure you are. Let me not pass you by
in quest of some rare and
perfect tomorrow."*

— Mary Jean Irion

■

Many people who have survived suicide attempts, or who have stopped themselves on the brink of suicide, have said how grateful they were to be alive!

■

*"Like a morning dream, life becomes
more and more bright the longer we live,
and the reason for everything appears
more clear."*

— Richter

■

They began to see that they needed themselves and that they did indeed have some worthwhile qualities — qualities like love, kindness, warmth, humor, caring, strength, wisdom, and many others.

"*You must not lose faith in humanity. Humanity is an ocean; if a few drops of the ocean are dirty, the ocean does not become dirty.*"

— Mohandas K. Gandhi

They began to see that even though there is ugliness, hate, indifference, and pain, there is also beauty, love, caring, and comfort.

Life is not all black and white — it's a mixture of good and bad.

"To do more for the world than the world does for you — that is success."

— Henry Ford

There are people who care for others just because *they are*. These people may not be part of your life right now, but they can be, if you reach out to them.

■

"The ultimate measure of a man is not where he stands in moments of comfort and convenience, but where he stands during challenge and controversy."

— Martin Luther King

■

Look for your strengths, not just your weaknesses.

Give yourself credit for enduring so much for so long.

"*Practicing love is the most important self-esteem tool for recovery, because when we practice love, we are making a connection with our real selves...making it clear that we are at our core, not flawed but divine. We realize we are truly worthy of self-esteem.*"

— Leigh Cohn and
Lindsey Hall

Don't focus on waiting to be loved.

Take action today and give just a little love to one person.

Everyone in the world wants to be loved. Be a source of love for someone.

■

"Most of us have a pretty clear under-standing of the world we want. What we lack is an understanding of how to go about getting it."

— Hugh Gibson

■

Look for your options.

You have choices.

Many more choices than just suicide.

■

*"It is important from time to time
to slow down, to go away by yourself, and
simply be."*

— Eileen Caddy

■

Get close to nature. Mother Earth is a great comforter.

Sit in the woods. Walk in a quiet, open meadow.

If you live in the city, walk in a park or go to the zoo.

"Learn to be silent. Let your quiet mind listen and absorb."

— Pythagoras

Sit quietly.

Concentrate on listening to the sounds around you — water splashing, leaves rustling, birds calling.

Allow the powerful peace of nature to enter your being.

Don't push it away, by trying to recall your troublesome thoughts. Just allow the natural tranquillity to come in.

Our bodies and minds will heal themselves in time, if we let it happen.

■

"The more sure you are, the more wrong you can be."

— Ashleigh Brilliant

■

If you are very sure that your problems are too huge to be overcome and there is no one at all who can help you, at least do one thing.

Call the teen-age crisis hotline.

The phone number is on page 220. The phone call is free.

Take a chance that the phone call might give you some new answers.

*"Be not anxious about tomorrow.
Do today's duty, fight today's temptations
and do not weaken and distract yourself
by looking forward to things you cannot
see and could not understand if you
saw them."*

— Charles Kingsley

Remember, suicide closes the door on new answers and second chances.

■

"Worry often gives a small thing a big shadow."

— Anonymous

■

If you are looking for peace, you can find it. But don't choose the cold, false "peace" of the grave.

Choose the warm peace of sitting in sunshine, listening to your favorite music, hugging a friend or someone who needs your hug.

"In every winter's heart there is a quivering spring, and behind the veil of each night there is a smiling dawn."

— Kahlil Gibran

The fog will clear.

The sun will shine and you will feel its warmth again.

Spring will follow winter.

Life will be good again and worth waiting for.

It will be worth living for.

■

*"Not until tomorrow will we see clearly
enough to appreciate the gifts of today."*

— Ruth Sargent

■

You are strong because you have endured so much. You can make it through one more day.

The fog just might lift tomorrow.

The sun could break through tomorrow.

There are so many good reasons for tomorrow.

■

"To keep our faces toward change and behave like free spirits in the presence of fate is strength undefeatable."

— Helen Keller

■

Wait till you can see tomorrow.

Wait.

You'll see.

-3-

You're Not Alone

Teens Talk about Handling Tough Times

You're Not Alone!

In the following section, you'll find short paragraphs that have been written by young people about how they felt when they went through a particularly tough experience or what they do when they're feeling down.

After each person's comments, on the following page are affirmations. Affirmations are simple, true statements that can help you build your self-confidence. Use these positive thoughts to replace the negative thoughts that run through your mind and reinforce your bad feelings about yourself.

It's a good idea to choose a few of the lines that are particularly meaningful to you. Write these affirmations on a piece of paper and put it on your dresser, desk, or at the edge of your mirror where you can see them at least once a day.

"The thing I worry about most is knowing when to...stop putting on a fake facade. I do this because sometimes I just don't feel good enough; like my regular self just doesn't please everyone....Maybe this is a common worry, maybe it's not, but it's just something that's been worrying me."

— April, 14

■ Deep inside I know that my real self is a good self.

■ The love I have to give is one of the things that makes me worthwhile.

■ Worrying about things is a natural part of life.

Today I will relax and be confident in the goodness of my real self.

"If I'm totally bummed out, like the time I wrecked my truck, I go over to my dad's house. He never says too much, except that I can stay as long as I want. When I feel better, I go back home."

— Cody, 18

■ I know I'm loved, even though the words aren't always said.

■ Giving time is a gift of love.

■ There are many kinds of love and many ways to say, "I love you."

Today I will give one gift of love — a hug to someone I love, a thank you to someone who's helped me, a compliment to my brother or sister.

"It sounds stupid, but I still sleep with my stuffed lamb. I'm too old, I guess, but my mom says it's okay. She says sometimes she feels like a little kid too."

— Sara, 17

■ Everyone has childlike feelings at times.

■ Feeling like a child isn't the same thing as acting like one.

■ The child in me deserves to be comforted.

Today I will give myself permission to have childlike feelings.

"When I'm stressed out, I like to sit by my grandmother. She always smells like powder and breathes slowly while she knits. Once in awhile she looks over and smiles a little, but mostly she keeps knitting and breathing. It almost makes me feel like I'm being rocked to sleep."

— Amelia, 14

■ Taking deep, slow breaths is a good way to relax.

■ Sometimes restful silence helps more than any words.

■ I can listen to silence and feel peaceful and at ease.

Today I will find a silent place to let energy enter my body and peaceful thoughts enter my mind.

"One day a long time ago, my oldest
brother said I wore stupid clothes. Then
my other brother said I acted so dumb he
could hardly believe it. But they were
always in bad moods and I usually feel
pretty good, so I decided to ignore them.
Now that I'm in high school, that's what I
do when older guys try to roust on me."

— Ryan, 14

■ I can handle criticism.

■ I will give myself credit for not getting down when people say negative things about me.

■ Learning to trust my own judgment gives me a sense of inner power.

Today I will remember to forgive others for hurting me and to forgive myself for not being perfect.

"My dog is my very best friend. When I get home from school, he's always waiting for me. Dogs never say they'll call you up later to make plans, then bail on you and go out with some other guys. They just love you all the time."

— Tyler, 16

■ No one can be a perfect friend, because no one is perfect.

■ When friends disappoint me, it doesn't mean I'm not good enough for them or that they don't like me.

■ I can learn to forgive and forget, releasing my bad feelings.

Today I will remember one of the times I felt best about myself and look forward to feeling those feelings again.

"My dad and I had a terrible fight once and I said, 'I wish you were dead!' For days after that, the words kept ringing in my ears. What if he really died! I was really getting freaked out. Then my mom saw me crying so I told her the whole thing. She said that saying bad things didn't make them happen. After that, I didn't worry about it so much. Finally, my dad and I made up."

— Kristi, 15

■ Everyone has frightening thoughts.

■ Thoughts are not the same as actions.

■ It's normal to get very angry with your parents.

Today I'll think about good qualities in each member of my family.

"When I was in the sixth grade, I cried in the shower every night for weeks because I was so scared to go away to camp. Camp turned out to be really fun and I was mad at myself for making myself so miserable. I decided that the next time I was that worried about something, I'd save it all up for the last three days before, so I wouldn't waste so much time."

— Mary, 14

■ The best way to deal with your fear
  is to face it.

■ Worry by itself won't fix anything.

■ Change the things you can. Accept the
  things you can't.

Today I will let my worries dissolve and
wash out of me.

"After we broke up, my girlfriend started acting really weird. First it was dumb stuff like getting hysterical at parties, so I'd have to take her home. Then she threatened to kill herself. I didn't know if she'd ever really do anything or not, but it still scared me. Finally, I told my aunt about it and she told my mother. My mother made me tell the girl's mother. That was so incredibly hard, but afterwards, I was really relieved. I guess the girl's okay now. I don't see her anymore."

— John, 18

■ Taking positive steps gives you a feeling of confidence in yourself.

■ When there's a serious problem, it's strong, not weak, to ask for advice.

■ Telling the truth is one kind of loving behavior.

Today I will believe in my strength and my abilities.

"One day my mom was really bugging me about my clothes. She has a thing about wanting me to dress like the preps, but I'm just not one of them. Finally, I said real softly so she wouldn't get mad, 'Mom, this is my life.' She looked at me sort of funny and smiled. I mean, what was she going to say, 'No, it's mine'? So, we talked about who gets to choose what in this family. I agreed to wear these certain dress-up shirts when we go out as a family, but then I get to choose what I wear to school."

— Bob, 13

■ Most people will listen if you give
  your opinion without getting angry.

■ You have the right to be your
  own person.

■ Healthy compromise with another
  person is not giving up.

Today I will believe in the good about
myself. I am becoming more confident in
myself every day.

Phone Numbers to Call
Youth Crisis Lines

■ "Metro-Help" is a toll-free, 24-hours-a-day, 7-days-a-week national crisis hotline for suicidal and runaway youths.

Call toll-free 1-800-621-4000.

■ Look under "Suicide Prevention" by alphabetical listing in the white pages of your local phone book. Most cities have suicide prevention hotlines staffed every day around the clock. Most of the phone numbers are toll-free.

■ The National Committee on Youth Suicide Prevention will refer you to the suicide prevention center nearest your home. They will also send you free information on youth suicide and prevention.

Write: National Committee on Youth Suicide Prevention, 67 Irving Place South, New York, New York, 10003.

Call: 1-212-677-6666.

■ The Youth Suicide National Center will mail you information and refer you to counseling.

Write: Youth Suicide National Center, 1825 I St., N.W., Suite 400, Washington, D.C., 20006.

Call: 1-202-429-2016.

Further Reading

Burns, David, M.D. *Feeling Good*. New York: Signet Books, 1981.

Hall, Lindsey and Cohn, Leigh. *Self-Esteem: Tools for Recovery*. Carlsbad, Connecticut: Gurze Books, 1990.

Hipp, Earl. *Fighting Invisible Tigers: A Stress Management Guide for Teens*. Minneapolis, Minnesota: Free Spirit Publishing Co., 1985.

Kennedy, Eugene. *If You Really Knew Me, Would You Still Like Me?: Building Self-Confidence*. Allen, Texas: Argus Communications, 1975.

Paul, Jordan, Ph.D. and Paul, Margaret, Ph.D. *If You Really Loved Me: For Everyone Who Is a Parent and Everyone Who Has Been a Child.* Minneapolis, Minnesota: CompCare Publishers, 1986.

Powell, John, J.S. *Why Am I Afraid to Tell You Who I Am?* Allen, Texas: Argus Communications, 1969.